Frank Kidder Upham

Genealogy and family history of the Uphams

Frank Kidder Upham

Genealogy and family history of the Uphams

ISBN/EAN: 9783337142469

Printed in Europe, USA, Canada, Australia, Japan

Cover: Foto ©Andreas Hilbeck / pixelio.de

More available books at **www.hansebooks.com**

GENEALOGY

AND

FAMILY HISTORY

OF THE

UPHAMS,

OF CASTINE, MAINE, AND DIXON, ILLINOIS,

WITH

GENEALOGICAL NOTES

OF

BROOKS, KIDDER, PERKINS, CUTLER, WARE, AVERY, CUR-
TIS, LITTLE, WARREN, SOUTHWORTH
AND OTHER FAMILIES.

COMPILED BY F. K. UPHAM, 1887.

PRINTED FOR PRIVATE CIRCULATION.
1887.

To the Posterity of John Upham.

THIS little book has been prepared for private circulation only. No apology is considered necessary for the printing of a work of this character; it is not for the public, and a record of honest respectability is all that is intended. By those whose family history, or any portion of it, is here shown, it is hoped it may be considered of sufficient value to insure its preservation, and possibly awaken further interest in the subject.

Of course it is not expected it will be read by many who are not themselves of the posterity; but it may be observed that the earlier pages, and to include the second generation in this country, are of common interest, and refer to ancestors which are equally those of all the American Uphams.

It has also be made to contain a reference to the known sources of further information, which might be useful to one engaged in preparing a like record of his own particular branch. A similar record to this is practicable in all the branches, and with the available material, is much less of an undertaking than will at first appear. This is the third one on the same plan which I have prepared for publication: that of Isaac Upham, of San Francisco, which was printed in 1884; and one which has not yet been printed, for Col. Chas. Leslie Upham, of Meriden, Conn. The publication of others is urgently recommended.

About ten years ago I began the collection of data, and had hoped to publish a complete genealogical record of all who bear this name, but have not met with sufficient encouragement to carry out the original purpose. This, if not abandoned, has been indefinitely postponed. To those who have furnished records, I wish to say that their labor was not a useless one; for all this material will be carefully preserved, and as opportunity offers, added to. With the steadily increasing interest in genealogical matters, no doubt it will eventually be utilized by some one representing the Uphams. The Rev. James Upham of Chelsea, Mass., has also an extensive genealogical collection, probably larger than any other.

F. K. U.

FORT CUSTER, MONTANA.
February, 1887.

GENEALOGY AND FAMILY HISTORY

OF A BRANCH OF

THE UPHAM FAMILY.

BY

FRANK KIDDER UPHAM, U. S. A.

JOHN UPHAM was the progenitor of all the American Uphams, so far as has been ascertained, either in the United States or British Provinces. He was born in England, somewhere between 1597 and 1600, probably in Somersetshire. His pedigree remains to be traced, though it is believed that it could be with the assistance of the data which is available.

The earliest authentic mention of the name Upham in England has been found in the Charter Rolls, in Turr, London, Vol. 1, Part 1, Folio 170, An. John, 1208. It is found in a deed of lands to the church of Saint Maria de Bradenstock, and is in substance that one Hugo de Upham conveyed, as a gift, certain lands from his estate to the church mentioned. Forty or fifty years later, in the Hundred Rolls, Temp. Henry III. and Edward I., Vol. 2, page 240, and still later in the Fine Rolls (during the reign of Henry III.), Vol. 2, page 376 (1246–1272), mention is found of several bearing this name, all of these of apparent local consideration. The name is also found in Doomsday Book, Vol. 2, page 36.

The church of Saint Maria de Bradenstock was a small monastery in Wilts, in the Hundred of Kinwarston, latitude 51° 23′, and longitude 1° 39′, west. All the individuals found on record were located so near this region that it is reasonable to believe they were of the same original descent. Indications also point to the probability that *John Upham's* pedigree could be traced to the same stock. What the origin of the family was it is difficult to base a theory upon; it may have been Saxon or Norman. At all events, it is shown to have been English for at least one generation, in the year 1208.

In the year 1845, Dr. Albert G. Upham, of Concord, N. H., published a little volume for private circulation, entitled, " Notices of *John Upham* and his Descendants," from which most of the above, as well as nearly all that follows of the life of *John Upham* and his son *Phineas*, has been taken. This book is of great interest in this connection, and should be read by all the Upham posterity. Besides this, an Upham genealogy, and matters pertaining thereto, have been published in the New

England Genealogical and Historic Register, Vol. 25, pages 13-15; Vol. 11, pages 45, 127, 211, 348; Vol. 12, pages 84, 239; Vol. 13, page 70; and in the January, 1879, number of the same was published an article entitled, " The name of Upham in England," the last mentioned having been prepared by the compiler of this genealogy, with the hope that it might sometime aid in eventually tracing the English origin of the American Uphams.

According to Camden Hotten's book on the early emigrants to New England, *John Upham* sailed from Weymouth, England, with his wife *Elizabeth* and three children, on the 20th of March, 1635, as one of a party of colonists which appears to have been organized in Somersetshire, and headed by a clergyman by the name of Joseph Hull; the said Hull having formerly been a rector in the established Church of England. The age of *John Upham* is given in this list as 35, at that time. After reaching America, he was prominent in the settlement of Weymouth, Mass., where the original colony located, and later in the settlement at Malden. At both these places he was a deacon in the church; and he was for several terms a member of the general court of the colony. He died at Malden, on the 25th of February, 1681; and according to the gravestone, which was last year still standing in the " Old Burying

Ground " at Malden,* he was 84 years old when he died. A discrepancy appears here between this and the age given in the list of passengers published by Hotten. Quite an extended account of *John Upham's* life in detail may be found in Dr. Upham's "Notices."

The name of his first wife was *Elizabeth*, probably *Elizabeth Webb*, as his brother-in-law appears to have borne that name, and may have come from the village of Badcome, in the county of Somerset, England. If so, *John Upham* probably came from the same locality. All of *John Upham's* children were by his first wife, though after her death (date not known) he married Catherine Holland, in August, 1671, she being one of the original party of colonists who came from England together.

Besides the " Notices," have been printed the Memoir of Judge Nathaniel Gookin Upham, 1871 ; a small book showing the ancestry of Isaac Upham of San Francisco, 1884; and the Memoir of Deacon Joshua Upham of Salem, 1885. Attention is also directed to the following books of reference where genealogical information showing various branches of Uphams may be found : Whitmore's American Genealogist, Bond's History of

---

* This gravestone was rapidly crumbling away as the time indicated, the inscription being read with difficulty. Unless some measures are taken to preserve it, it will soon disappear entirely. Doubtless the posterity would gladly contribute to the erection of a suitable monument, if any one of the descendants would initiate a movement to that end.

Watertown, Farmer's Genealogical Dictionary, Lincoln's Worcester, Barry's Framingham, Draper's Spencer, Freeman's Cape Cod, Washburn's Leicester, The Bi-Centennial Book of Malden, Durrie's Pedigrees, and a Manuscript Upham's Genealogy, left incomplete by Thomas B. Wyman, at his death. All of which can be found at the New England Society's House in Boston. An examination of the pages of these works will lead the enquirer to nearly, if not quite all, that has been placed on record concerning this genealogy and family history up to the year 1887.

John Upham, and his wife *Elizabeth* (*Webb?*) had the following children:

1. John, born in England, age 7, when family left England, as per Hotten; died young.
2. Nathaniel, born in England, age 5, when family left England, afterward a Minister of Cambridge; died without children.
3. Elizabeth, born in England, age 3, when family left England, the wife of Thomas Welsh.
4. *Phineas*, who was probably born very soon after the family reached America. The scriptural significance and association of the name leave no doubt that he was the "first born" on this side of the Atlantic and consequently the first American Upham.
5. Mary, born in Massachusetts, the wife of John Whittemore.
6. Priscilla, born in Massachusetts, the wife of Thomas Crosswell.

PHINEAS UPHAM (No. 4, preceding family) married *Ruth Wood*, who died at the age of 60, in 1696-7. He was prominent in Malden, and in the settlement of Worcester, Mass.; was a lieutenant in the Indian War with King Philip; was wounded on the 19th of December, 1675, at the storming of the Narragansett Fort Canonicus, from the effects of which wound he died on the following October, 1676. A very interesting and full account of the life of this ancestor may also be found in the " Notices."

In the January, 1886, Genealogical and Historic Register, will also be found an interesting account of the battle of Fort Canonicus with the wounding of *Lieut. Upham.* The General Court of the Colony voted a pension to his family after his death.

Phineas Upham and wife *Ruth Wood* had—

1. Phineas, born 1659.
2. Nathaniel, born 1661.
3. Ruth, born 1664; died age 12.
4. John, born 1666.
5. Elizabeth, who married Samuel Green.
6. *Thomas*, born about 1668.
7. Richard.

THOMAS UPHAM, of Reading, Mass. (No. 6, preceding family), is once mentioned as a weaver, and appears to have been interested in a mill at Reading, where he owned property.* He may also have been interested

---

* The north part of Malden, including ten families, was annexed to Reading, 1729. This annexation included the Green, Upham, and Evans families, and was the part which is now Greenwood; that which was situated southerly of the old Smith farms.

with his brother Richard in the "Upham farm," at that place. He died in his 67th year, November 28th, 1735. His first wife was Elizabeth Hovey, of Topsfield, whom he married in 1693, and who died, age 32, February 16th, 1703-4. He married for his second wife Mary Brown, of Reading, October 2d, 1704, who died in 1707. He married for his third wife *Ruth* (widow of John Smith, of Charlestown), daughter of *Thomas Cutler*, of Reading. She was born in 1688 and died May 12th, 1758, in her 70th year. Her grandfather, *John Cutler*, came from Norfolk County, England, to Hingham, Mass., 1637. *Thomas Cutler*, third son of *John*, age 40 in 1675, married *Mary Giles*, 1659-60, and lived at Reading; their third child *Ruth*, born February 2d, 1668, was the wife of *Thomas Upham*.

They had—

1. Thomas, born 1694, baptised at Topsfield, November 18th.
2. Elizabeth, born 1695.
3. Abijah, " 1698.
4. Nathan, " 1701.
5. Josiah, " 1705, of Weston, son of second wife.
6. *Joseph*, " 1712, of Dudley, son of third wife; died in 81st year, 1792.

JOSEPH UPHAM (No. 6, preceding family), born at Reading, 1712, died at Dudley, October 12th, 1792, in his 81st year. His earlier life was passed at Reading, but he moved to Dudley about the year 1748 with his wife and five children. He was apparently a man of means at that time, which may have accumulated at Reading, or which may have come to him, in part, through his father (*Thomas*). He purchased a tract of land in the northeast part of Dudley, containing some 450 acres, and settled his sons around him in later years upon different portions of this estate. Four pieces of this property which had been so divided were in the possession of the Upham's at Dudley in 1878, who still retained the original deed. He was one of the early settlers, and the Uphams are of the original families at Dudley. He married first Martha Green, of Malden, on the 20th of November, 1732, who died September 11th, 1738. He married second, *Elizabeth Richardson*, of Woburn, February 28th, 1739. She was the granddaughter of *Samuel Richardson*, of Woburn, and was born December 4th, 1715. She died, after the birth of all his children, and he again married at the age of sixty-four, in January, 1777, Abigail Amsden, a widow.

His children were—

1. Martha (daughter of Martha Green), born May 6th, 1738. Married Thomas Wilson, of Killingly, Conn., October 18th, 1759.
2. *Joseph* (son of *Elizabeth Richardson*), born December 10th, 1740.
3. Thomas, born December 10th, 1742. Married Elizabeth Pratt, of Oxford, February 19th, 1784.
4. Elizabeth, born February 14th, 1745. Died at Dudley, October 28th, 1831.
5. Susanna, born April 15th, 1747. Married David Kidder (son of *Richard*), February 23d, 1758.

All the above born at Reading, the others at Dudley.

6. Benjamin, born September 14th, 1749. Married Hepzibah Larned November 20th, 1778. Revolutionary soldier, called out at the Lexington alarm, 1775. Died June 16th, 1827; age, 62.

7. Ruth, born December 30th, 1751. Died at Dudley; unmarried; age, 65.

8. Lois, born May 18th, 1754. Married Philip Brown, September 28th, 1775.

9. Simeon, born May 11th, 1757. Married Miriam Larned, June 22d, 1785. Died 1847. A Revolutionary soldier.

10. Nathan, born June 8th, 1763. Married Mary Robins, March, 1797, who died in 1846. He died November 6th, 1847.

Samuel Richardson, of Woburn, and his wife *Joanna*, had two sons, *Samuel* and *John*. *Samuel*, the eldest son, and his wife *Martha*, had a son *Samuel* born in 1670. *John*, the second son, married *Eliza Bacon*. They had a son *John*, who married *Susanna Davis*, and they had a daughter, *Susanna Richardson*. *Samuel Richardson*, 3d, born in 1670, married his distant cousin, *Susanna Richardson*, born January 6th, 1703-4. They had *Elizabeth Richardson*, who was the second wife of *Joseph Upham* and the mother of all but the first of his children.

JOSEPH UPHAM, JR. (No. 2, preceding family), born at Reading, December 10th, 1740, came to Dudley with his father when about eight years of age, remaining at· Dudley, probably on the old place, during the remainder of his life ; date of his death not known. He married at Dudley, April 16th, 1765, *Eunice Kidder*, who was born December 7th, 1735, the daughter of *Richard Kidder*, whose (*Richard's*) grandfather, *James Kidder*, came from England and settled at Cambridge, Mass., before 1650, where he married (about 1649) *Anna*, the daughter of Deacon *Francis Moore*, a leading citizen of Cambridge at that time. *James Kidder* was a descendant (sixth generation) of *Richard Kidder*, who lived at Maresfield, County Sussex, England, in 1492. See record and genealogy of Kidder's following.

The children of *Joseph Upham, Jr.*, and his wife *Eunice*, all born at Dudley, were—

1. Eunice, born September 24th, 1766. Married Charles Brown, September 11th, 1788.
2. Joseph, 3d, born October 14th, 1769. Married Susanna Jewell, of Oxford, April 15th, 1791, at Dudley. He died at the age of 55 and she died at the age of 72, in New York, to which State they removed soon after their marriage. They had children, Joseph, Jeremiah, Jared, Susan, Gratia, Clarissa and Fanny. Descendants living at Black Creek, New York, and vicinity.
3. Jeremiah, born May, 1771, who committed suicide by hanging.
4. Hannah, born May 13th, 1774. Married Abel Rogers, of Castine, and died at Dixon in 1856. She was the mother of Mrs. Joshua G. Pinckney, who also died at Dixon, and had children, Eugene, a lawyer of Dixon; Charles, of Denver; Micajah, of California; Delia, Frank, and Hannah Jane, deceased.
5. Elizabeth, born March 18th, 1776. Married Davis Larned, October 17th, 1802.
6. *Sylvanus*, born February 6th, 1788. Settled at Castine.

SYLVANUS UPHAM (No. 6, preceding family), settled at Castine about the year 1800, being, consequently, 21 or 22 years of age at that time. He appears to have left his father's people in Massachusetts and never returned to them; his sister Hannah also went to Castine. His wife claimed that he was heir to certain property at Dudley, which was never received. In early life he was said to have been a person of unusual ability and strength of character, and carried on the business of a carpenter and builder at the time when Castine was in its most flourishing condition. He is mentioned in Wheeler's History of Castine as among those who had money in 1810. He was a believer in the Unitarian system of religion, and seems to have held independent views upon matters generally, so far as his son, *Sylvanus Kidder*, could remember. While still comparatively young, he was attacked by a fever, from the effects of which he never recovered, though he lived some years afterward. His wife stated that, owing to malpractice by his physician, Dr. Mann, his mental faculties were injured, and remained in an impaired condition during the remainder of his life, during which time he was no longer able to enter upon, or control the active business affairs of former years. He died at Castine, March 8th, 1830, aged 52. The means which had been accumulated in early life had been mostly expended at the time of his death, owing to the misfortune which had followed in later years. From a portrait which remains in the possession of his descendants he appears to have been a man of medium size, brown hair, sharp hazel or brown eyes, strongly marked and well-defined features, with a very positive expression of countenance. The general effect of this portrait has been compared to that of a minister of the olden time. His wife was *Mary Avery*, whom he married at Castine, May 17th, 1802. She was the daughter of *Thatcher* and *Hannah* (*Atkins*) *Avery*, and a descendant of *Dr. William Avery*, who came to Dedham, Mass., in 1650, from Barkham, Berkshire County, England, and who was a descendant (fourth generation) of *Robert Avery*, of Pyle, County of Somerset, England. *Dr. William Avery* is buried in King's Chapel Ground at Boston. The Averys were a very respectable New England family, whose members had been largely composed of doctors and clergymen. *Thatcher Avery* (father of *Mary*) was born at Truro, Mass., February 15th, 1757; married *Hannah Atkins* (daughter of *Nathaniel*, of Truro, born 1739, died at North Castine, 1825; wife, *Mary Staples*) August 19th, 1779, and settled at North Castine, where he owned a large farm and hotel—"tavern," as it was called in those days—old "Avery House," still standing, and a landmark in that section. *Thatcher Avery* was a Major in the Militia, and known as "Major Avery" throughout the surrounding country, in which he was a very popular and well-known person in his day. During the war of 1812, Castine was occupied by the British troops, and a number of the officers were "quartered" upon *Major Avery*, who became a great favorite with them personally on account of hospitality and good fellowship. Among the valuable relics in the family which have descended to these times is a set of china, with the monogram of Major Avery and wife on each piece. Also the old-style cups which were used by the British officers. Tradition informs us, however, that notwithstanding the Major's popularity with these officers he was extremely patriotic, and never became quite reconciled to the presence of his enforced guests ; that on more than one occasion, when "the cup that cheers" had freely circulated, his patriotic sentiments were stronger than his discretion, and he expressed himself so plainly and forcibly that they were glad to bring matters to an arbitrary close. *Mary Avery* (daughter of above) was born at Truro, April 8th, 1783 ; died at Castine, June 18th, 1859, aged 76 years.

Sylvanus Upham and wife, *Mary*, had—

1. Hannah, born May 17th, 1803, who married John Clifton, of Salem, where she died, age 35; leaving children: Hannah Upham (wife of Benjamin P. Ware, of Marblehead), born at Castine, September 16th, 1823; Sarah Helen, born at Salem, November 8th, 1828 (wife of John Payne, of Connecticut); they have a daughter Helen, the wife of E. B. Taylor, architect, of Boston; John Quincy Adams, who died at Boston, 1885.
2. Jeremiah, who married Cornelia Crawford, October 27th, 1831, at Castine, and had: Cornelia Adams, who married James B. Osgood, of Ellsworth, Me., and lives at Washington, D. C.; Susan, who died in Boston, December, 1878; James Crawford, born about

2

1839, living at Sydney, Cape Breton, Nova Scotia. Jeremiah Upham, died on the Island of Zanzibar, Africa, 184-, while on a voyage to that country.

3. *Sylvanus Kidder*, born at Castine, March 11th, 1811.

SYLVANUS KIDDER UPHAM (No. 3, preceding family), received an English education in his native town, and was first engaged in the leather business at Castine, but finding it unprofitable with the decline of trade in that town, about 1843-4, he moved to Boston with his family, which consisted of a wife and two children. At Boston he entered into partnership with his brother-in-law, J. B. Brooks, and engaged in the West India goods trade on Long Wharf; and was later in the commission business. On the discovery of gold in California, he became one of a Boston company which purchased the brig "Colonel Tayloe," loaded it with merchandise suited to the California mining trade, and on the 14th of February, 1849, sailed from Boston, *via* Cape Horn for California. After a tedious voyage of more than seven months, they reached San Francisco on the 21st of September, 1849. He was successfully engaged in business in California for about eighteen months, at Sacramento, Coloma and Georgetown, and then returned to his family which had been living at Salem during his absence. He then purchased a home at Woburn, and was for a short time again in business at Boston, but found nothing quite satisfactory. In

1853 he sold out, went West, and settled at Dixon, Illinois, where his brother-in-law and several others from Castine, who were friends and relatives of both himself and wife, had preceded him. At Dixon he engaged in the lumber business, at that time being obliged to have his entire stock brought in rafts down Rock River, as railroads had not yet reached Dixon. He continued in this business for many years, and up to within a few years of his death, which occurred at Dixon on the 13th of February, 1883, at the age of nearly 73, caused by an abscess of the bowels, from which he had been suffering for some time, but had been unable to determine the cause.

In appearance, he was of medium stature, about five feet six inches high; weighing perhaps 140 pounds; a fair complexion and blue eyes; of a very active temperament, which never permitted him to be without constant employment of some character. After retiring from business in 1874, his time was mainly occupied in reading, having an especial taste for all scientific subjects, and classical literature, which an active business life had heretofore prevented him from gratifying.

In his earlier years he had been a member of both the Congregational and Presbyterian Churches, and was at one time a deacon in the Congregational Church at Dixon, but after the death of his wife his interest in religion was not manifested. He died as he had lived, respected by those who knew him, an honest and an honorable man.

The estimation in which he was held by his fellow-citizens perhaps is best shown by the following extracts from the daily papers at the time of his death. The first is from the *Dixon Telegraph* of February 15th, 1883 :

" Again we are called upon to record the death of an old resident and highly respected and much beloved citizen of Dixon. S. K. Upham died at his home in North Dixon, Tuesday morning, after a protracted illness, extending over many months. The funeral services will take place at the residence this morning at ten o'clock. Mr. Upham was born in Castine, Maine, March, 11th, 1811, and became a citizen of Dixon about thirty years ago. He was, a number of years, in the lumber trade here, a partner at the time of Mr. Charles F. Emerson, of this city—the firm name was Upham & Emerson—but he retired from business some time since. Last summer he took a trip to the Southwest in hopes to improve his failing health, but, receiving no benefit, returned in a few weeks, and was confined to his house after that time. S. K. Upham had the respect and esteem of all who knew him. He was a gentleman of excellent literary taste, well educated, and possessed of a mind cultured much above the average business man. We have read several bright and sparkling productions from his pen, and we have often thought that had it not been for a peculiar modesty which characterized him he would have made his mark in the literary world. Genial and generous in his nature, he was a pleasant companion, a good neighbor and a valued citizen. The deceased leaves a widow and three children: Capt. Frank K. Upham, Mr. Charles Upham and Mrs. Margaret Wright. The latter has been several years in Europe engaged in literary pursuits ; and the two sons are in the West, one in the army, and the other engaged as civil engineer for the Atchison and Santa Fe Railroad. The death of Mr. Upham will cause a pang of deep regret in many a heart, and his good cheer will be missed upon our streets."

The second, from the Dixon *Sun*, of February 14th, 1883: "After a long and painful illness, Mr. S. K. Upham died yesterday morning of internal tumor, at the age of 72. He was born in Castine, Maine, March 11th, 1811. He went to California in 1849, and, after a year and a half spent there, returned to his home in the East. He came with his family, consisting of wife and four children, to Dixon in 1853, and has been actively engaged in business up to within the past few years. Several years ago he lost a married daughter, and subsequently his first wife. He leaves a widow, two sons and a daughter. During his long business career no man in Dixon has made more sincere friends and fewer enemies. His kindness of heart and sterling good qualities have endeared him to the hearts of all who came into close relation to him. The funeral services will be conducted at the family residence, in North Dixon, at 10 o'clock to-morrow."

The wife of *S. K. Upham* was *Marianne Brooks*, who was born at Castine, January 11th, 1819, and died at Dixon on the 30th of December, 1870, aged almost 52 years. They were married at Castine on New Years Day, 1839, and had she lived one day longer would have completed thirty-two years of married life. She was the daughter of *Barker* and *Margaret (Perkins) Brooks*, and a descendant (in the sixth generation) of *William Brooks*, who came to Scituate, Mass., from England, in 1635, as one of the passengers of the well-known ship "Blessing." His descendants have continued at Scituate, Dorchester and South Boston until the present time; the male representatives through various generations being mostly either sea captains or ship builders. *Barker Brooks* (father of *Marianne*) was born at Scituate on the 10th of September, 1789, and was a ship builder. He was early in the ship building business at Boston, and came to Castine on business connected with that interest when a young man; finally he engaged in permanent business at Castine, which was then a very flourishing seaport, where ship building was a very important industry. He married *Margaret Perkins*, July 16th, 1816, and continued in business at Castine until he died, March 16th, 1838, in his forty-ninth year; his death having occurred through an accidental injury which brought on an internal abscess. The Brooks shipyard was a large and important one, where many of the best ships of New England were built; one of which was the good ship "Adams" of which John Holmes, one of the sons of *Barker Brooks*, became captain at the age of 21. Some of the older people of Castine, who remembered *Barker Brooks*, have described him as tall and dignified in appearance, of a light complexion, and whose kind and genial disposition, combined with strict integrity and correct business habits, gained to him the respect and esteem of the entire community. In common with his father's people in Massachusetts, he appears to have held Unitarian views concerning religion, while his wife was a member of the Congregational Church, and on Sunday mornings, by a mutual agreement, the children were divided: the father taking the boys with him to the Unitarian Church, and the mother taking the girls with her to her own church.

Margaret Perkins, the wife of *Barker Brooks*, and the mother of *Marianne* (*Upham*), was the youngest of ten children; she was born at Castine on the 19th of April, 1790, and died January 30th, 1838, aged 47; her death occurring, as may be observed, but a few weeks prior to that of her husband, and from a cause which was somewhat similar in its nature to that which caused the death of her husband, though of a different origin. We are told that she was a kind and devoted wife and mother, and that her strength of character was unusual. The latter, with the advantage of the good social position which was occupied by both her own and her father's family, may have strengthened the aristocratic tendencies which have been attributed to her, and which seem to be apparent in the portrait which her descendants now have. By this, at all events, we learn that she was very handsome, with clear-cut, regular features, and dark hair and eyes. Her father was *Captain Joseph Perkins*, a wealthy man and large ship owner. He was one of the three original proprietors of the peninsula upon which Castine is located. A long account of him with, a record of his family, is printed in Wheeler's History of Castine. Through this ancestor the descendants have, or believe they have, at the present day, an interest in the French Spoliation Claims.

Marianne (*Upham*) in person resembled her father, was tall, of fair complexion, with blue eyes and light brown hair. Having been well endowed by nature, and receiving a good education in her youth, her mental attainments were considerable and her usefulness was great.

The following obituary notice appeared in one of the papers at Dixon, and was written by the Rev. E. C.

Sickles, for many years pastor of the church of which she was a member, and who also delivered a funeral address which was very gratifying to the family. He had known her long and well.

" DIED—Friday, December 30th, of acute enteritis, Mrs. Marianne Upham, wife of S. K. Upham, Esq., aged nearly 52 years.

" Mrs. Upham was born in Castine, Maine, where she passed the greater part of her life before her removal to this place in 1853. For nearly eighteen years, therefore, she has been known among us, winning by her graces of character and person a large number of loving friends. She was gifted by nature with a strong mind and a lovely disposition, and had attained a high degree of culture, so that her loss is deeply felt by all who knew her. It was religion, however, that invested her character with its greatest charm. For many years she was a member of the Congregational Church in her native place, and latterly of the Presbyterian Church here, and she was more than a consistent Christian, she was a cheerful, happy one, adorning her profession and commending, by her beautiful life, religion to all.

" Her mind readily received the truths of revelation and her heart fully rested in them. The result was a strong Christian character, peace and cheerfulness constantly. At home she diffused happiness. 'The heart of her husband trusted in her, and her children rise up and call her blessed.' Of her numerous friends and acquaintances, many were in the habit of resorting to her for counsel and comfort in times of perplexity and trouble, so reliable was her judgment, and so full of sympathy her heart.

"Some three years since the shadow of a great affliction rested upon her and hers, in the loss of a lovely daughter, a favorite, too, in the church and community, but resultant, as all her friends could see, were the 'peaceable fruits of righteousness,' and a rapid ripening for glory.

"During her short illness her entire household were present. The elder son, an officer in the regular army, after an absence of more than eleven years on the Western frontier, had returned on leave of absence but a few weeks previous, and a younger son, absent for several months, had come home to pass the holidays. Certainly, it was a remarkable providence that, after so long a separation, brought them together around the sick and dying bed of a mother, and it was a source of very great comfort to her.

"The nature of her illness was such as to produce much suffering and extreme prostration, but she retained the use of her faculties to the end. She gathered the family around her, and gave to each words of counsel and blessing. Frequent were her expressions of peace and joy during the hours of waning strength ;

rendering her dying like her life, calm and beautiful. To one, who asked if the Saviour were present, she replied, ' Oh, yes; I have trusted him long, and he is no stranger to me now.' To another, who, when near her end, remarked: ' You are almost there, aren't you?' she said, ' Yes, and it thrills me with joy when I can fully realize it."

" Much more she said of like import, until, at last, quietly and gently she ' fell on sleep.'

> " ' She is not tasting death, but taking rest
> On the same holy couch where Jesus lay;
> Soon to awake all glorified and blest,
> Where day is broke, and shadows fled away.'

"Sabbath, the 1st inst., was the 32d anniversary of her marriage. On that day, her funeral was attended from the Presbyterian Church, which was filled to overflowing with sincere mourners."

On the 12th of August, 1872, *Sylvanus Kidder Upham* married Mrs. Angelina Sewell, widow of the Rev. Daniel Sewell, who survived his death.

Sylvanus Kidder Upham and wife *Marianne Brooks*, had :

1. Margaret Barker, born at Castine, November 19th, 1839.
2. *Frank Kidder*, born at Castine, May 30th, 1841; compiler of these notes.
3. Annie Gay, born at East Boston, Mass., August 20th, 1845; married Edward Utley, at Dixon, November 27th, 1866; died— -at Dixon, June 12th, 1867.

28

4. Charles Clifton, born at Woburn, Mass., May 5th, 1852; a civil engineer. Chief Engineer Chicago, Burlington and Northern Railroad, living at St. Paul, Minn., in 1887. Married at Dixon, December 18th, 1883, Anna St. John Eells, who was born at Dixon, November 6th, 1860; daughter of Samuel Cook Eells (born at Walton, Delaware County, N. Y., March 19th, 1822), and his wife, Anna Elizabeth Moore (born at Delhi, N. Y., September 1st, 1835). Samuel Cook Eells, descendant of Nathaniel Eells, who came from England, and settled in Dorchester, Mass., 1634, and whose descendant Nathaniel, settled in New York.

At the completion of the Chicago, Burlington and Northern Railroad, an account of the building of the road was published in the Dubuque, Iowa, *Times*, of the 31st October, 1886, wherein the following mention of Charles C. Upham was made.

THE CHIEF ENGINEER.

The man who holds the theodolite, the gentleman who manipulates the transit instrument—in fact, the man who is the scientific head of a great railroad enterprise, is more or less the subject of admiration of the uneducated populace. To bring a great railroad to completion requires more brains, more education and more general ability than most people are aware of. The very first commencement of a new railroad must be entrusted to the engineers, who have made a study of that particular branch. A railroad engineer has always certain problems to consider, for which he must be fortified by a careful technical education. Mr. Charles C. Upham was born in Woburn, Mass., thirty-four years ago. He entered the railroad service in 1872, and from that time until 1875 was connected with the Grand Junction, Bellville and North Hasburgh Railroad. For three years after that time he was a mining engineer in Colorado. In 1878 he became connected with the engineering corps of the Atchison, Topeka and Santa Fe Railroad; extending his operations to the central branch of that road which ran to the southwest, toward Mexico. In 1884 Mr. Upham joined the engineering corps of the Chicago, Burlington and Quincy Railroad. From that time until August, 1885, he continued in that position, when he accepted a place as Chief Engineer of the Chicago, Burlington and Northern Railroad, a great amount of this road's success being due to his scientific labors.

Margaret Barker Upham (No. 1, preceding family), married at Dixon, November 22d, 1859, Dr. Zalmon James McMaster, who was from Auburn, New York. He died at the age of 31, while surgeon of an Illinois regiment—during the war of the rebellion—from sickness contracted in the line of duty, by exposure while caring for the wounded on the battle-field after Pittsburg Landing; on account of which a pension was given by the Government to his wife and child. He was the son of Hugh J. McMaster, who died at Auburn, on the 31st of March, 1876, aged 75. The Mc-Masters, a very respectable family of Scotch descent, which settled in the Mohawk Valley and vicinity before the Revolutionary War. (Alonzo D. McMaster, of Rochester, New York, has genealogical records of this family).

Margaret Barker married June 24th, 1868, Charles Henry Wright, of Chicago, who was born at Deposit, Delaware County, New York, June 24th, 1838. He was a journalist, and at the time of his death at Chicago, on the 10th of September, 1869, was city editor of the Chicago *Times*. He was a young man of unusual ability and promise, and very popular with the members of the Chicago press, who published a pamphlet. "In Memoriam," at his death, copies of which are still extant. Margaret Barker, now living at Cambridge, Mass., a contributor to current magazine and other literature as Margaret Bertha Wright, and for a time represented the *Art Amateur* and other American publications in Europe. She has children:

1. Marian Lois, born at Eureka, Illinois, July 21st, 1861, daughter of Dr. McMaster, though her name has been legally changed to Marian Lois Wright. An artist in oil painting.
2. Charles Henry Conrad Wright, born at Chicago, November 16th, 1869, ten weeks after the death of his father. Employed on the Cambridge *Tribune*.

FRANK KIDDER UPHAM, (No. 2, preceding family), Captain First United States Cavalry, married at Dixon, April 1st, 1871, *Sarah Elvira Camp*, who was born at Filmore, Montgomery County, Illinois, November 23d, 1852. Daughter of *Harvey Camp*, who was born at Hanover, New Hampshire, December 10th, 1820; his wife, *Susan Southworth*, born at Bradford, Vermont, March 8th, 1823. They were married in 1844, and removed to Illinois soon after. The Camps, originally from Milford, Conn. Nicholas Camp was in Milford, 1639, and was married July 14th, 1652. (For which and other reference to Camps, see Savage's Gen. Dic., Vol. I., page 331.) The Southworths settled early at Duxbury, Mass. (See pedigree of Southworth following).

Frank Kidder and wife, *Sarah Elvira Upham*, have:*

1. Frank Brooks, born at Fort Apache, Arizona Territory, September 7th, 1872.

2. John Southworth, born at Fort Walla Walla, Washington Territory, November 5th, 1881.

3. Ethelberta, born at San Francisco, California, February 9th, 1883.

4. Edith, born at Fort Walla Walla, Washington Territory, May 17th, 1884.

BOUND FOR NEW ENGLAND.

[Reprinted from John Camden Hotten's "Original Lists of Persons of Quality; Emigrants; Religious Exiles, &c. who went from Great Britain to the American Plantations, from 1600 to 1700."]

WAYMOUTH ye 20th of March, 1635*

1. JOSEPH HALL, of Somers' a Ministr aged 40 year
2. AGNIS HALL his Wife aged........25 yr
3. JOANE HALL his daught' aged 15 Yeare
4. JOSEPH HALL his sonne aged 13 Yeare
5. TRISTRAM his son aged.........11 Yeare
6. ELIZABETH HALL his daught' aged 7 Yeare
7. TEMPERANCE his daught' aged 9 Yeare
8. GRISSELL HALL† his daught' aged 5 Yeare
9. DOROTHY HALL† his daught' aged 3 Yeare
10. JUDETH FRENCH his s'vamt aged 20 Yeare
11. JOHN WOOD his s'vaunt aged 20 Yeare
12. ROBT DABYN his s'vamt aged 28 Yeare
13. MUSACHIELL BERNARD of batcombe Clothier in the County of Somersett 24 Yeare
14. MARY BERNARD his wife aged 28 yeare
15. JOHN BERNARD his sonne aged 3 Yeare
16. NATHANIELL his sonne aged 1 Yeare
17. RICH: PERSONS salter & his s'vant: 30: yeare
18. FRANCIS BABER Chandler aged 36 yeare

*[Really 1635-6.]   †[So in the original.]

19 JESOPE Joyner aged 22 Yeare

20 WALTER JESOP Weaver aged 21 Yeare

21 TIMOTHY TABOR of Som's' of Batcombe in
    taylor aged 35 Yeare———————

22 JANE TABOR his Wife aged 35 Yeare

23 JANE TABOR his daugh" aged 10 Yeare

24 ANNE TABOR his daught': aged 8 yeare

25 SARAH TABOR his daught' aged 5 Yeare

26 WILLM FEVER his s'vaunt aged 20 Yeare

27 JNO WHITMARCK   aged 39 yeare

28 ALCE WHITMARKE his Wife aged 35 yeare

29 JMO * WHITMARKE his sonne aged 11 yeare

Portus
Waymouth 30 JANE his daught' aged   7 Yeare

31 OUSEPH [or ONSEPH] WHITMARKE his sonne
    aged 5 yeare

32 RICH: WHYTEMARK his sonne aged 2 Yeare

33 WILLM READ of Batcombe Taylor in

34† Som's" aged 28 Yeare——— ————

35 SUSAN READ his Wife aged 29 Yeare

36 HANNA READ his daugh" aged 3 yeare

37 LUSAN‡ READ his daught' aged 1 yeare

38 RICH: ADAMS his s'vante 29 Yeare

39 MARY his Wife   aged 26 yeare

40 MARY CHEAME his daught' aged 1 yeare

41 ZACHARY BICKEWELL   aged 45 Yeare

42 AGNIS BICKWELL his Wife aged 27 yeare

43 JNO BICKWELL his sonne aged 11 year

---

*[Sic. But doubtless intended for JOHN.]

†[It will be noticed that No. 34 is placed against the name of a place instead of that of a person.]

‡[Probably intended for SUSAN.]

3

44 Jno Kitchin his servaunt   23 yeare

46* George Allin   aged 24 Yeare

47 Katherin Allyn his Wife aged
        30 yeare————————

48 George Allyn his sonne aged 16 yeare

49 Willm Allyn his sonne aged 8 yeare

50: Mathew Allyn his sonne aged 6 yeare

51 Edward Poole his s'vaunt aged 26 yeare

52 Henry Kingman   aged 40 Yeares

53 Joane his wife beinge aged 39

54 Edward Kingman his son aged 16 year

55 Joane his daught' aged 11: yeare

56 Anne his daught' aged....9 Yeare

57 Thomas Kingman his sonne aged 7 Yeare

58 John Kingman his sonne aged 2 yeare

59 Jn Ford his servaunt aged 50 Yeare

60 William Kinge   aged 40† Yeare

61 Dorothy his wife   aged 34 yeare

62 Mary Kinge his daught' aged 12 year

63 Katheryn his daught' aged 10 Yeare

64 Willm Kinge his sonne aged 8 year

65 Hanna Kinge his daught': aged 6 year

66‡ Somm'. [Somerset.]

        Thomas Holbrooke of Broudway aged 34: yeare

67 Jane Holbrooke his wife aged 34 yeare

68 John Holbrooke his sonne aged 11 yeare

69 Thomas Holbrooke his sonne aged 10 yeare

70 Anne Holbrooke his daught' aged 5 yea[re]

---

*[There is no 45.]

†[Or 30. One figure is written over the other, and I cannot tell which is the later.]

‡[Thus in the original. This number should evidently come against the next line.]

71 ELIZABETH his daught' aged 1 yeare

72 THOMAS DIBLE husbandin aged 22 yeare

73 FRANCIS DIBLE soror aged   24 Yeare

74 ROBERT LOVELL husbandman aged 40 yeare

75 ELIZABETH LOVELL his Wife aged 35 yeare

76 ZACHEUS LOVELL his sonne 15 yeares

78* ANNE LOVELL his daught': aged 16 yeare

79 JOHN LOVELL his sonne aged 8 yeare

ELLYN his daught' aged .... 1 yeare

8o JAMES his sonne aged........1 yeare

81 JOSEPH CHICKIN his servant 16 year

82 ALICE KINHAM aged........22 yeare

83 ANGELL HOLLARD aged .... 21 yeare

84 KATHERYN his Wife 22 yeare

85 GEORGE LAND his servaunt   22 yeare

86 SARAH LAND† his kinswoman 18 yeare

87 RICHARD JOANES of Dinder.........

88 ROBT MARTIN of Badcombe husbandm 44

89 HUMFREY SHEPHEARD husbandm..32

90 JOHN VPHAM husbandman ....35....

91 JOANE MARTYN.................44....

92 ELIZABETH VPHAM...............32....

93 JOHN VPHAM Jun................07....

94 WILLIAM GRAUE [GRAVE]..........12....

95 SARAH VPHAM....................26....

96 NATHANIELL VPHAM.............05....

97 ELIZABETH VPHAM...............03....

Dors' RICHARD WADE of Simstuly

98‡ Cop [Cooper] aged...............60....

*[There is no No. 77; but it will be observed that two lines below there is a name without a number.]   †[Originally written LANG.]

‡[This number should be in the line above.]

99   Elizabeth Wade his Wife....... 6*....

100: Dinah his daugh'................22....

101 Henry Lush his s'vant aged   17....

102 Andrewe Hallett his s'vaunt   28....

103 John Hoble husbandm ....13....

104 Robt Huste husbandm ....40....

105 John Woodcooke .... 2....

106 Rich Porter husband............ 3....

JOHN PORTER Deputy
Cleark to EDW:
THOROUGHGOOD.

The foregoing names are those who have been known
at Weymouth as the "Hull Colony." Joseph Hall,
whose name heads this list, is the Joseph Hull of Weymouth. His descendant, Joseph B. Hull, of New York,
thinks this colony was composed of West Country people, and came principally from that point in England
where the counties of Somerset, Dorset, and Devon
join. Several are known to have come from Broudway
in Somerset.

John Upham is also mentioned in "News from New
England."

Gilbert Nash, of Weymouth, Mass., has written an
extremely interesting paper concerning the early settlement of Weymouth. It was printed in the *Weymouth
Gazette* of February 23d, 1883, after having been read
before the Weymouth Historical Society and the Ge-

---

* Sic. in orig.]

neological Society at Boston. From this it appears that " Mr. Hull was born in Somersetshire, England, about the year 1590; was educated at Oxford University, St. Mary's Hall, where he graduated in 1614; became rector at Northleigh, Devon, in 1621, which position he resigned in 1632, when he commenced gathering from his native county, and those surrounding it, the company with which he sailed from Weymouth, Dorset, March 20th, 1635. Savage says ' Mr. Hull came over in the Episcopal interest,' and his sympathies seem to have leaned in that direction, although while in America he was professedly a non-conformist, or Independent."

John Upham's name also appears quite conspicuously in the same paper.

The Rev. Joseph Hull afterwards returned to England, and was, in 1659, Rector of St. Buryan's, Cornwall, though he again came to New England, where he died at the Isle of Shoals in 1665.

CUTLER FAMILY.

John Cutler came from Sprawston, Norfolk County, England, to Hingham, Mass., in 1637. His widow *Mary* sold land there in 1671.

They had, third son—

Thomas Cutler, age 40 in 1675, who died September or December 7th, 1683. He married in 1659 or 1660, *Mary Giles*.

They had—

Ruth Cutler, born at Charlestown, Mass., February 2d, 1668 or 1669, who first married John Smith, May 18th, 1693, who died in 1705, leaving three children. She married second, *Thomas Upham*, at Reading.

KIDDER FAMILY.

A full history and complete genealogy of this family from 1492, to present generation is printed in "Kidder's History of New Ipswich," New Hampshire, published in 1852; also in the "History and Records of the Kidder Family," published in 1876, by Rev. Samuel T. Kidder, of Beloit, Wisconsin, completed to year of publication, with Coat of Arms of Kidders, etc.; also a still more full "History of the Kidders," by F. E. Kidder, of Alston, Mass., 1886.*

1. *Richard Kidder* and wife lived at Maresfield, County Sussex, England, in 1492.
2. *Richard Kidder*, second, died in 1653, at Maresfield.
3. *John Kidder*, son of *Richard*, second, died at Maresfield, 1599.
4. *John Kidder*, son of *John*, was baptized at Maresfield, 1561, and died 1616.
5. *James Kidder*, son of *John*, was baptized at East Grinstead, County Sussex, England, in 1595.
5. *James Kidder*, son of *James*, was born in East Grinstead, in 1626, came to New England, and settled at Cambridge, Mass., before 1650: he died at Billerica, Mass., April 16th, 1676. He married, probably about 1649. *Anna*, the daughter of Deacon *Francis Moore*, one of the leading and most influential citizens of Cambridge at that time. They had twelve children, among whom was:
7. *Ephraim Kidder*, son of *James*, born August 31st, 1660: died at Billerica, September 25th, 1724. He married *Rachel Crosby* at Billerica, in 1685.
8. *Richard Kidder*, son of *Ephriam*, born at Billerica, May 10th, 1705; settled at Dudley, Mass. His wife's name was *Hannah*. They had the following children, composing the Ninth Generation, born at Dudley:

   a. Rachel, born October 8th, 1729; married Jessie Dimerick, May 19th, 1751.
   b. Hannah, born November 8th, 1731; married Alexander Brown, August 17th, 1775.
   c. Samuel, born February 8th, 1734; married Sarah Corbin, March 30th, 1758.
   d. *Eunice*, born December 7th, 1735; married *Joseph Upham*, at Dudley, April 16th, 1765.

---

* Susanna Kidder, one of this family (daughter of the English Bishop of Bath and Wells, Richard Kidder) married Sir Richard Everard, Bart., one of the early governors of North Carolina. Descendants in Virginia, among whom: Hon. Richard Kidder Meade, and the Episcopal Bishop of that State, Kidder M ade.

e. Richard, born May 9th, 1738.'

f. David, born June 28th, 1740; married Susanna Upham, February 23d, 1768.

g. Nathaniel, born August 29th, 1746; died December 9th, 1756.

h. Thomas, born August 21st, 1750.

The American Kidders use a Coat of Arms, which differs from that given in Burke's General Armory, and which is as follows: "Kidder (Marsefield, Co., Sussex, temp. Henry VII.) Vert, three crescents, or, crest: A hand couped, below the elbow vested, az. holding in the hand ppr. a packet, thereon the word 'Standard.'"

AVERY FAMILY.

This family originated at Pyle, County Somerset, England, where the Coat of Arms of the family was thus described (Hart, Mss. 1144): "Gules, Cheveron between three besants, or, crest: Two lions gambs, or, supporting besant."

1. *Robert Avery*, of Pyle, is the earliest ancestor to which the line has been traced.

2. *William Avery*, of "Cougnsbury (?)," Somerset, England, son of *Robert*.

3. *Robert Avery* (son of *William*), of Workingham, Berks, England.

4. Doctor *William Avery* (son of *Robert*), came from Barkham, Berkshire County, England, and settled at Dedham, Mass., in 1650, with his wife *Margaret*. He died March 18th, 1686-7. His tomb-

stone was standing in King's Chapel ground, Boston, in 1879. They had children in the

Mary, baptized December 19th, 1645.

William, baptized October 27th, 1647.

Robert, baptized December 5th, 1649, and four other children who were born at Dedham.

SIXTH GENERATION.

Reverend *John Avery* (son of *Robert*, baptized December 5th, 1649), was born in Dedham, February 4th, in 1685 or 6. He was graduated at Harvard University in 1706, and ordained as a minister in Truro, Mass., 1711 (for further, see Freeman's History Cape Cod and Riche's History Truro, Mass). He married, November 23d, 1710, *Ruth*, the daughter of *Ephraim* and *Mary Little*, who was born at Marshfield, Mass., November 23d, 1686. (See Little Family.)

SEVENTH GENERATION.

Job Avery, of Truro, was the seventh son of Rev. *John Avery*, and was born at Truro, on Monday, about 4 A. M., January 14th, 1722–3. There were ten children in this family.

EIGHTH GENERATION.

Thatcher Avery, was the seventh of the children of *Job Avery;* he was born in Truro, February 15th, 1757; married *Hannah Atkins*, August 19th, 1779, and settled at North Castine, Maine, where he was a prominent citizen, owned a farm and hotel; was also Major in the Militia, and known as "Major Avery." *Hannah Atkins*, his wife, was born at Truro, May 27th, 1766, and died at Castine, December 20th, 1828; she was the daughter of *Nathaniel Atkins*, who was born at Truro in 1739, and died at North Castine in 1825, and his wife, *Mary Staples*, of Truro.

The children of *Thatcher* and *Hannah* comprise the

NINTH GENERATION.

1. Hannah, born at Truro, June 4th, 1780; the wife of William Freeman; she died September 26th, 1799.

2. *Mary*, born at Truro, April 3d, 1783; married at Castine, May 19th, 1802, *Sylvanus Upham*; she died at Castine, June 18th, 1859.

3. Thatcher, born February 14th, 1785.

4. Jane, born January 12th, 1787; married John K. Blodgett.
5. Prudence, born September 14th, 1790; died September 23d, 1799.
6. Elizabeth, born April 25th, 1793.
7. Ruth, born April 10th, 1795; married Elisha Chick, of Frankfort, Maine.
8. Samuel, born March 22d, 1797; lost at sea, August 1st, 1811.
9. Sally, born April 2d, 1797; married Oliver Parker.
10. John Atkins, lived at North Castine; born February 20th, 1802; died 1873.
11. Isaiah, born February 16th, 1806; lived at Exeter, Maine, where he had a large family; died August 16th, 1872.

LITTLE FAMILY.

1. *Thomas Little*, emigrant from England, settled in Plymouth as early as 1630, and is said to have been a lawyer. He married in 1633, *Ann*, daughter of *Richard Warren*, of Plymouth. *Richard Warren* came to this country in the "Mayflower," 1620, leaving in England his wife *Elizabeth* and five daughters, who followed him three years later in the ship "Ann," William Pierce master. His two sons, Nathaniel and Joseph Warren, were born at Plymouth. The name of Richard Warren, the Pilgrim, is found in the "Mayflower" list of passengers in Prince's Chronology. In the same book his death is recorded thus: "1628. This year dies Mr. *Richard Warren* a useful instrument, and bear a deep

share in the difficulties attending the settlement of New
Plymouth." The Plymouth Colony Records contain
frequent references to *Richard Warren* and members of
his family. Volume VIII, page 35, has the following
record of the death of his wife: "Mistress *Elizabeth
Warren* an aged widdow aged 90 years deceased on the
second (?) of October 1673, who having lived a Godly
life came to her grave as a shoke of corn, fully ripe.
She was honorably buried on the 24th of October
aforesaid."

Thomas Little and wife removed in 1650 to Marsh-
field. He died March 12, 1671. Their children were:
Thomas, killed by Indians in Rehoboth fight, 1676;
Samuel, who married Sarah Gray; *Ephraim;* Isaac,
born about 1646; Hannah, married Stephen Tilden;
Mercy, married John Sawyer in 1666; Ruth, and
Patience. Both *Ephraim* and Isaac had descendants,
among whom was the distinguished Capt. George
Little, U. S. Navy. The family was conspicuous in Ply-
mouth, Marshfield and Scituate, for several generations.

2. *Ephraim*, son of *Thomas* (1), born in Marshfield
May 17, 1650. He married, in 1672, *Mary*, daughter of
Samuel Sturtevant, of Plymouth, and had children, viz.:
Ephraim, born 1673, graduated at Harvard College
1695, and became minister at Plymouth; Ruth, born
1675, died soon; David; John, born 1683; *Ruth*, born
Nov. 23, 1686, married Nov. 23, 1710, *John Avery*, son

of *Robert* and *Elizabeth* (*Lane*) *Avery* of Dedham; Ann, and Mary; and perhaps others. He died Nov. 24, 1717. She died February 10, 1717, and were both buried at Scituate. (See Avery Family preceding.)

BROOKS FAMILY.

William Brooks, the progenitor of all the Brooks family in this line, came to Scituate, Mass., in the ship "Blessing," John Lemister, Master, in the year 1635. He was then aged 20 years. His brother Gilbert, age 14, came with him to Scituate.

William Brooks was at Scituate in 1644, and his farm was south of "Tilles," afterward "Dudley's Creek." The place in England from which the Brooks brothers came has not been ascertained. Many Scituate families came originally from Yorkshire, some of the earlier settlers from County Kent, and it is probable that the Brooks family may have originated in one of these localities. The name may have been originally spelled "Brookes" or "Brooke." *William Brooks* married widow *Susanna* Dunham, of Plymouth; their house was situated near the spot upon which Captain William Brooks' house stood (his descendant in the sixth generation), and seems to have been selected for the clear

spring water which flows near it. (Foregoing items
from Deane's History, Scituate, 1831, and Barry's History, Hanover, 1853.)

The children of *William* and *Susanna Brooks*, above
mentioned, were :

Hannah, born 1645.
Nathaniel, born 1546, who married *Elizabeth*, the daughter of *Richard Curtis* (See Curtis Family), in the year 1678, and succeeded to his father's estate, and from him all the Scituate Brooks descended, who lived there in 1831.
Mary, born 1647.
Sarah, born 1650; married Joseph Studley.
Miriam, born 1652; married John Curtis, son of *Richard Curtis*.
Deborah, born 1654; married Robert Stetson, Jr., son of the Cornet.
Thomas, born 1657; married Hannah Bigsby, 1687.
Joanna, born 1659.

The sons of *Nathaniel Brooks* above, who married
Elizabeth Curtis, were :

William, Gilbert, *Nathaniel second.*
Nathaniel second, married *Mary Taylor* in 1717, and purchased lands of Michael Wanton, one-half mile west of the "Hoop pole Hill" where his descendants are still living at Scituate. He left children, among whom there is the record of
Nathaniel third, who married Elizabeth Benson in 1744, and *Taylor*, who married *Miriam Curtis* in 1740.

There were probably other children of whom there is
no satisfactory record.

Taylor Brooks and *Miriam*, his wife, may have lived
at Hanover, and probably did in 1750, as it is found in

Barry's History of Hanover that Taylor Brooks, a ship builder, was living there at that time. The only child of the above found on record is—

Captain *Noah Brooks*, born 1744, and who died at sea.

Captain *Noah Brooks* above had children, among whom (if not all of whom) were—

1. Captain Noah Brooks, of South Boston, who married Hannah Stetson, of Scituate; descendants living at Dorchester. He was a ship builder and a wealthy man.
2. *Barker Brooks*, born at Scituate, September 10th, 1789.
3. Thomas Brooks, married and settled at Alfred, Maine. (His children were: Raymond, Charlotte, Barker and Sarah; Charlotte married for her second husband, Josiah Little, of Portland, and settled at Lewiston, Maine.)
4. Nancy, married William Bradford, of Kingston.
5. Hannah, married Samuel Kent, of Scituate.
Another daughter who married Hon. John Holmes, of Maine.

Barker Brooks (2d son of *Noah* above) was also a ship builder; he married *Margaret Perkins* (see Perkins Family) July 16th, 1815, and settled at Castine, Maine, where he died March 16th, 1838, and where his wife, *Margaret*, also died, January 30th, 1838. Their children, all born at Castine, Maine, were—

1. Phebe Perkins, born April 8th, 1817; married Benjamin D. Gay, who died at Dixon, Illinois, 1857. They had: James, who died young, and twins, Sarah and Mary; the latter died in November, 1880; Phebe Gay and daughter Sarah living at Newburyport, Mass.
2. *Marianne*, born January 11th, 1819; married at Castine, January 1st, 1839, *Sylvanus K. Upham*; she died at Dixon, Illinois, December

30th, 1870, children: Margaret Barker, *Frank Kidder* and Charles Clifton.

3. Joseph Barker, born August 15th, 1820; married at Dixon, Illinois, January 1st, 184-, Ophelia Loveland, of New York State. He died at Dixon, December 21st, 1855. She died at Dixon, 187-, leaving Margaret Adelaide, Henry James (now M. D. at Dixon).

4. James Otis, born July 25th, 1822; married Sarah F. Abbott, of Maine, September 8th, 1847, at Lawrence, Mass. He died September, 1847, at Lawrence, leaving no children.

5. Margaret Perkins,   ) Twins, born October 20th, 1824. Margaret
6. Sarah Holmes,   ) Perkins died January 10th, 1826. Sarah Holmes died June 21st, 1826.

7. John Holmes, born April 24th, 1828. Sea Captain. He died at Philadelphia, November 17th, 1880, and was buried at Castine. He married Mary Westcott, of North Castine, 185-. They had one child, Walter, who died, age about 12; widow living at Newburyport.

8. Noah Brooks, born October 24th, 1830. Married Caroline A. Fellows, at Salem, Mass., May 29th, 1856. She died at Marysville, California, 1862.

The following personal notice is taken from *The Book Buyer*, published in New York:

NOAH BROOKS.—Mr. Brooks was born in the old-fashioned and quaint-looking town of Castine, Maine, in 1830, of good old Massachusetts stock. He sallied forth at the age of 18 to make his own way in the world. At first educated to be an artist, he felt around for his right place (after the manner of our American youth) some time before he found it. Boston, the literary Boston of 1850, gave him his first start in journalism, and that, too, of the best sort, for in those days the young journalist, though scantily paid, was rooted and

grounded in the principles of successful literary en-
deavor. When 24 years old, the young and budding
writer struck out for what was then the far West, and
in Illinois tried his hand most unsuccessfully at mercan-
tile pursuits. Next, in company with a devoted band
of "Free State" enthusiasts, he took up his line of
march for the Territory of Kansas, then convulsed with
civil war. The war over, and the hare-brained farming
experiment of the young adventurers (for there were
two of them) being a failure, the twain moved on to
California, in one of the revivals of the early gold fever.

In California, the old instinct of journalism being
strong in him, Mr. Brooks started a daily paper in partnership with two other enthusiastic Republicans, and
the *Appeal*, published in Marysville, Yuba County, was
a lively sheet in the hands of Messrs. Avery & Brooks,
the senior partner of the concern being Benjamin P.
Avery, afterward United States Minister to Pekin, a
gentle and refined writer of much ability and vigor.
Suffering loss of family in the sudden death of wife and
only child, Mr. Brooks recrossed the continent in 1862
and established himself in Washington as correspsond
ent of the great leading California paper of those days-
the Sacramento *Union*. As "Castine," the well-known,
correspondent, Mr. Brooks won fame for himself all
over the Pacific States. An intimate friend of Lincoln
for many years, he was offered the post of private sec-

retary to the President and was ready to take the place when the good President was slain.   Once more recrossing the continent, Mr. Brooks was commissioned Naval Officer of the port of San Francisco.   Soon after he returned to the newspaper, the *Alta California*, of San Francisco, securing his services as managing editor.   Anon, in 1871, he returned eastward and took the place of night editor of the New York *Tribune*, thence to the *Times*, where he held his place as editorial writer from 1875 to 1884, when he migrated across the Hudson to become editor of the Newark (N. J.) *Daily Advertiser*, and where he remains at this present writing.

In all these wanderings, Mr. Brooks has been a busy man.   Of a social and jovial disposition, he has formed it is said, more acquaintances than any man of his years not in what is called public life.   But in the legitimate field of his work Mr. Brooks has been indefatigable.   In San Francisco, for example, he wrote stories, sketches, and book reviews for the *Overland Monthly*, while Bret Harte was editor of the exceedingly lively magazine; conducted a semi-monthly publication for young people, sent letters to Eastern journals, wrote editorials, and superintended the daily work of the *Alta California*.

Very early in the history of *Scribner's Monthly*, he contributed short stories to that periodical.   His first story, by the way, "The Cruise of the Balboa," pur-

4

ported to be an account of the seizure of a merchant ship by her cargo of Chinese coolies, the massacre of the crew and all the officers but the captain, who, fortified in the cabin, held the wretches at bay, and was an unwilling voyager during the months of drifting that passed before the ship, having circumnavigated the Pacific Ocean, arriving in Japan. The story was told with so much realism and apparent sea-lore as to "deceive the very elect;" and more than one seafarer wrote to the amused author for additional particulars; and one writer actually contributed to the archives of the Navy Department a report of certain "additional facts, which, as an officer of the navy, had come under his observation." The explanation of all this was that there was one grain of fact in the bottom of this volume of fiction. In another story, "Lost in the Fog," contributed to the *Overland Monthly* and subsequently printed in Charles Scribner's Sons' "Stories by American Authors," Mr. Brooks drew a similar realistic sketch, this time of a Spanish town unknown to, and unknowing, the American conquerors of California, on the lower coast of the State. This was absorbed into the current history of the times, so that, years after, somebody writing a biographical sketch of the author, soberly said that he had been cast away in a fog, and · had made some remarkable antiquarian discoveries.

Of another *Overland Monthly* story, "The Honor of

a Family," Mr. Brooks tells an odd experience. Afflicted with insomnia, he had been advised to try bromides as a soporific. The drug invariably caused vivid but not unpleasant visions. Once he dreamed a scene, like a tableau, in which the characters of a small domestic drama were grouped, and an exciting dialogue took place. Upon waking, he thought over the vision with great interest as suggesting a story. Falling asleep again, he actually dreamed another scene, in which appeared all the characters of the first tableau, but the action anticipated that of the first part of the vision. Next day, remembering vividly both these disjointed sketches, he combined the two, invented a connecting plot, and from these materials evolved what proved to be a capital story.

But Mr. Brooks' favorite field is that of fiction writing for young people. In his story of the " Boy Emigrants," published in New York in 1876 and in London in 1878, Mr. Brooks has wrought over his experiences and adventures on the plains, crossing to California. In the " Fairport Nine," published in 1880, he gave his boy readers a glimpse of the hearty, happy life of his own youth in Castine, thinly veiled under the title of " Fairport." In the " Life of Abraham Lincoln," for young people, which, it is understood, Mr. Brooks is now writing, we shall find of course many leaves from his experience in Washington during the war.

CURTIS FAMILY.

Many Scituate families came originally from Yorkshire, England; some of the earlier settlers of Scituate
came from Tenterden in Kent. The Curtis family
descended from *Stephen Curtis*, of Appledore, Kent,
about 1450. Can be found in Berry's Genealogies.

CURTIS ARMS:

"Argent, a cheveron, sable, between three bull's heads,
cabassed gules. Crest: A unicorn pass, or, between
four trees, ppr."—*Berry's History Hanover.*

Richard Curtis was one of four brothers, who came
early to New England, viz.: *Richard*, Thomas, John,
and William.

Richard had lands at Marblehead, Mass., in 1648, and
in the same year he purchased lands in Scituate, and
built a house between Goin's, White's and the harbor.
He married *Lydia*, in 1649, and had children:

Amos,   born 1649.
Elizabeth   "   1651.
John,   "   December 1st, 1653.
Mary,   "   1655.
Martha,   "   1657,
Thomas,   "   March 18th, 1659.
Deborah,   "   1661.
Sarah,   "   1663.

He died 1693. His daughter *Elizabeth* (above) married *Nathaniel Brooks* in 1678. *Miriam Curtis*, who
married *Taylor Brooks* in later generation, 1740, was
also of this family.

PERKINS FAMILY.

Jacob Perkins, of Old York, Maine, was born about the year 1695 ; it is probable that he was of the Ipswich, Mass., Perkins family. The family was prominent among the early settlers at York.

Joseph Perkins, descendant of *Jacob*, married *Abigail Wardwell*, who was the daughter of Elder *Ephriam Wardwell*. *Joseph* and *Abigail Perkins* had :

1. Jedediah.
2. Pelatiah.
3. *Joseph*, who was born at Old York, October 19th, 1746, a sea captain. He married *Phebe Ware*, at York, April 29th, 1770 (O. S.). He finally settled with others from Old York at Castine, Maine, being one of the largest original land owners, and most wealthy, influential citizens of that place. A long account of him is printed in Wheeler's History of Castine. He died at Castine, August 20th, 1818, (N. S.) His wife, *Phebe Ware*, was born at Old York, December 16th, 1748, and died at Castine, August 20th, 1815.

They had—

1. Mary, born at York, December 27th, 1771; died December 3d, 1833.
2. William, born at York.
3. Joseph, born at York, July 28th, 1774.
4. James, born at York, March 26th, 1776; died September 12th, 1815.
5. Dolly, born at Majorbagaduce (North Castine), June 15th, 1779; died November 3d, 1856.
6. Ebenezer, born June 8th, 1781; sea captain; died July 26th, 1827.
7. Rufus, born at Majorbagaduce, June 4th, 1785; died 1818.
8. Phebe, born in Penobscott (North Castine), April 12th, 1787.
9. Abigail, born in Penobscott, November 8th, 1788.

10. *Margaret*, born at Castine, April 19th, 1790; married *Barker Brooks* of Castine; died at Castine, January 30th, 1838.

Wheeler's History of Castine, published in 1875, has full history and record of Perkins among the "Old Families."

WEARE OR WARE FAMILY.

PETER WEARE was living at York, Maine, in 1652, was a lawyer by profession, and signed the submission to Massachusetts in that year. He is said to have come to New England between 1634 and 1640, and to have gone to York from Hampton, New Hampshire. He is also said to have been the most prominent man at York about this time. He may have been a brother or cousin to Robert Weare, of Dedham, whose posterity is given in the January, 1877, number of the N. E. Genealogical and Historic Register, but there is no proof of this, nor is his ancestry known. It is possible he may have come from the family of Weare (Were or Ware) which has been in Devonshire and Somersetshire, England, since the fourteenth century. Several of the names appear in the local histories who were identified with the Parliamentary cause in the Civil War. The family started in Yorkshire, but in reward for services at Crecy and Poitiers land was granted to them in the

Western counties. (See Burke's Landed Gentry and County Families.)

Elias Weare was the son of *Peter*. He died between 1706 or 7 and 1711, and is believed to have been killed by Indians, August 10th, 1707, with three others. His wife was *Magdelon* Adams, nee *Hilton*, who afterwards married John Webber, and had a daughter Hannah, born September 18th, 1711. There was a Magdelon Adams, of York, Me., on a list of English captives who were ransomed at Quebec, in October, 1695, by Matthew Carey, which was quite likely this *Magdelon Adams*, and whose maiden name appears to have been *Hilton*.

Joseph Weare was the 5th child of *Elias* and wife *Magdelon*. He was born March 17th, 1704-5, and died at the age of 87, in 1791 or 2. He married *Mary Webber*, who was born April 15th, 1710. She was the third of eleven children of *Samuel Webber* and wife *Elizabeth*, the daughter of Deacon *Rowland Young*. The father of this *Samuel Webber* was also *Samuel*, and he was killed by Indians in 1712 near York Hill.

Phebe Weare was the daughter of *Joseph* and wife *Mary (Webber)*. She was born at York, December 5th, 1748 (O. S.), and was the youngest of ten children, which number she also appears to have been the mother of. She married Captain *Joseph Perkins*, of York, April 29th, 1770, (O. S.) They settled at Castine, where she died Aug. 20, 1815, (N. S.) This name in later generations is spelled Ware.

(The heads of the generations of Ware which remained at York, and followed after *Joseph*, the father of *Phebe*, were Jeremiah, Jeremiah, William and Stephen.)

NOTE.—The following pedigree is taken from "A Genealogical Sketch of the Families of the Rev. Worthington Smith, D. D., and Mrs. Mary Ann (Little) Smith of St. Albans, Vermont," compiled by Captain Edward Worthington Smith, U. S. A., and published in 1878. Captain Smith says : " The information afforded by the following pedigree was mainly collected in England, in 1851, by Dr. J. C. Warren, who has since published an elaborate book on the subject. The facts, as given by him, are accepted as authentic by reputable works on kindred subjects, and are, so far as I can learn, undisputable."

LINEAGE OF RICHARD WARREN, OF PLYMOUTH, EMIGRANT BY THE "MAYFLOWER," 1620.

(1.) William de Warrenne, Earl of Warrenne in Normandy, and first Earl of Surrey, a near kinsman of William the Conqueror, held immense possessions in England, the reward of his services at the battle of Hastings. He married Gundred, or Gundreda, daughter of King William, and resided at the castle of Lewes, in Sussex.

(2.) William, son of William (1), second Earl of Warrenne and Surrey, married Isabel, daughter of Hugh,

Earl of Vermandois, and died May 11, 1138. His eldest son, William, the third Earl, died a Crusader in Palestine without male issue, leaving the title to his daughter Isabel.

(3.) Reginald, second son of William (2), married Adela, daughter of Roger de Mowbray.

(4.) William Warren, son of Reginald deWarrenne (3), married Isabel, daughter of Sir William de Hayden, Knight.

(5). Sir John, son of William (4), married Alice, daughter of Roger de Townshend, Esquire.

(6.) John, son of Sir John (5), married Joan, daughter of Sir Hugh de Port, Knight.

(7.) Sir Edward, son of John (6), married Maud, daughter of Richard de Skeyton.

(8.) Sir Edward, third son of Sir Edward (7), married Cicely, daughter of Nicholas de Eaton, Knight.

(9.) Sir John, son of Sir Edward (8), married Agnes, daughter of Sir Richard de Wynnington, Knight.

(10.) Sir Lawrence, son of Sir John (9), married Margery, daughter of Hugh Bulkley, Esquire, of Ware, in Shropshire.

(11.) John, son of Sir Lawrence (10), married Isabel, daughter of Sir John Stanley, Knight.

(12.) Sir Lawrence, son of John (11), married Isabel, daughter of Sir Robert Leigh, Knight.

(13.) William, second son of Sir Lawrence (12), seated

at Counton, Nottinghamshire, married Anne ———:
died 1496.

(14.) John, son of William (13), married Elizabeth
———; died 1525.

(15.) John, second son of John (14), of Headbury,
Parish of Ashburton, Devonshire.

(16.) Christopher, son of John (15).

(17.) William, son of Christopher (16), married Ann,
daughter of John Mable, of Calstocke, Cornwall.

(18.) Christopher, son of William (17), married Alice,
daughter of Thomas Webb, of Sidnam, Devonshire.

(19.) Richard, fourth son of Christopher (18), of
Greenwich, Kent, married Elizabeth Juatt (or Jewett),
and came to Plymouth in the " Mayflower," 1620. His
children were:

> Nathaniel, married Sarah Walker.
> Joseph, married Priscilla Faunce.
> Mary, married Robert Bartlett, of Plymouth.
> Ann, married Thomas Little, of Plymouth.
> Sarah, married John Cooke, Jr., of Plymouth.
> Elizabeth, married Richard Church.
> Abigail, married Anthony Snow.

Although I have attempted to do so by considerable correspondence, I have been unable to prove, or
to satisfactorily disprove this remarkable pedigree;
and have, therefore, decided to preserve it here for
future reference, with a view to its ultimate comparison
with the original sources of information. Proof is

wanting that Elizabeth, the wife of Richard Warren, the Pilgrim, was Elizabeth Juatt, relict of Marsh; or that he was the son of these two. After which that John, of Headburg (No. 15), was son of John (No. 14), who died 1525, and his wife Elizabeth. Dr. J. C. Warren, of Boston, Professor at Harvard University, first published this information in 1854; the material for which had been collected by Mr. Somerby, a reliable genealogist, and it was arranged by Dr. Warren for publication.

NOTE—The following pedigree is a transcript from the history of Duxbury, Mass., and is inserted here for future reference and preservation in connection with the genealogy of the particular branch of American Southworths to which reference is made in the pages of this book; the genealogy of which, in this country, yet remains to be traced.

SOUTHWORTH.

(1.) Sir Gilbert Southworth of Southwick Hall, in Lancaster, Kent, Knight, married Elizabeth, daughter and sole heir of Nicholas Dagis of Salmsbury, Lancashire, England.

(2.) Sir John Southworth, son of Sir Gilbert (1), of Southworth, Kent, married Elizabeth, daughter of John Haughton, Lancashire.

(3.) Sir Thomas Southworth, son of Sir John (2), married Jane, daughter of John Boath of Barton, Esq.

(4) Richard Southworth, son of Sir Thomas (3), of Salmsbury, Esq., married Elizabeth, daughter of Edward Molineaux of Sigtow, Esq.

(5). Sir Christopher Southworth, son of Richard (4), of Southworth, married Isabel, daughter of John Dalton of County Chester.

(6.) Sir John Southworth, son of Sir Christopher (5), of Salmsbury, Knight, married Ellen, daughter of Richard Langton of Newton Walton, Lancashire.

(7.) Sir Thomas Southworth, son of Sir John (6), heir to titles and estates; Christopher Southworth, second son; Richard Southworth, third son.

(8.) Christopher Southworth, second son of Sir Thomas (7), of London, merchant, married Jane, daughter of Edward —— of Shropshire.

(9.) Henry Southworth, son of Richard (8), was living in Co. Somerset, England, with wife Elizabeth, in 1623; Thomas Southworth, second son, recorder of wills in Somerset, married Jane, daughter of Nicholas ——.

(10.) Constant Southworth, son of Thomas, second son of Henry (9), married Alice Carpenter, who after death of her husband, Constant Southworth, went to Plymouth, Mass., and married Governor Bradford.

(11.) Thomas Southworth, of New England, son of Constant (10), married Elizabeth Raynor; Constant Southworth, second* son of Constant (10), married

* It is not quite clear whether Constant was the second or first son, as the dates of birth are not recorded.

Elizabeth ———. It is understood that from this Constant and wife, Elizabeth Southworth, have descended all the American Southworths.

Kingman's History of North Bridgewater, Mass., page 650, says: "Widow Alice Southworth came to Plymouth in the ship Ann, August 1st, 1623. Her two sons, Constant and Thomas arrived in 1628, both of whom became distinguished citizens in the old colony. The widow married Governor Bradford."

It is a matter of history that Gov. Bradford lost his first wife by drowning while on the way from England, and later, after reaching here, sent to England for the widow Alice (Carpenter) Southworth, whom he married after her arrival at Plymouth.

Although, as already stated, the record is wanting to connect this line, there appears to be no doubt the Vermont Southworths are of the original Plymouth and Duxbury family. It is remembered that in about 1838–40, there was a Southworth genealogy in existence at West Fairlee, Vt., which "ran back to a very early date," but I have been unable to obtain any trace of it by recent inquiry. Below is what has been obtained from those now living.

Ralph Southworth lived either at or in the vicinity of West Fairlee and died in 1842. His wife died in 1851-2 They had—

1. Ralph.
2. Elisha.
3. Eunice, married David Baldwin, who died at West Fairlee about 1843, leaving a large family, among whom Dr. David Baldwin, of Oakland, California.
4. Horace.
5. *Joseph*, who married *Susan Jenkins.*
6. Phineas, who married and had Algernon, Laura, and a younger son.
7. Irena.
8. Phydelia.

Joseph Southworth, of West Fairlee, Vermont, and wife *Susan Jenkins*, had—

1. Pamelia.
2. Joseph.
3. Edmond C. (living in Kansas.)
4. *Susan*, born at Bradford, Vermont, March 8th, 1823; married *Harvey Camp.* These are the parents of *Sarah Elvira Camp*, who married *Frank K. Upham*, as shown in preceding pages.
5. Elizur, born at West Fairlee, Sept. 22, 1826; living at Litchfield, Illinois; a lawyer. Elected State Senator in 1876; served four years. Elected again in 1884; term to expire in 1888.

"THE LANDS OF JOHN UPHAM."*

" 1636. At a meeting of the town of Weymouth, holden the 12th of June, Voted, That for the great lotts we should lott unto every complete person six acres. And to every half passenger, under twelve years of age, to have three acres to a head, by all the freemen here present whose names are under written; and the place to begin is at the lower end of the fresh pond, and to run eighty four rods towards the great lotts plantation."

In the list of fifteen names which follow the above John Upham's name appears with a grant of 30 acres, of which the following is an exact copy :

" Fower acres in king-oke-hill first given to himself, Bounded on the east with Edmond Parkers land, on the west by a highwaie, Mr. Webb's land on the north, Thomas Rawlings on the south; Two acres in Harris Rainge, Thomas Cleftenes lands on the East; a highwaie on the west, the lands of Walter Harris on the north, of John Burrye on the South; Two acres of salt marsh, with a little Island adjoining it, called Burryinge Island, Mr. Newmans lands on the East, the sea on the west, Enoch Hunts on the South; Thirty acres in the greatt lotts—the pond on the east—the common on the west—Stephen West on the North."

---

* From Weymouth, Mass., Town Records, Vol. i. pages 25, 27.

NOTE.

With a view to eventually tracing the origin of John Upham, of Weymouth, I have from time to time inserted queries in the *New England Historic and Genealogical Register*, the last of which is in the July (1886) number. To these should be added the following item : " *The Genealogist*, New Series, Vol. III., page 97, Visitation of Dorsetshire, 1565 ; Lovell of Tarrant Rawston *alias* Antyocheston Dorset. Jane, daughter of John Lovell, married to *Richard Upham*. (No date, but before 1565, probably as early as 1500.)

5

ERRATA.

Page 9.—Add Savage's Genealogical Dictionary to list of reference books.

Page 14.—Sylvanus Upham was born 1778, instead of "1788," as printed.

Page 22.—In line at bottom of page year 1816, should be 1813.

Page 44.—Twelfth line from bottom, "Dudley's Creek," should be Dwelley's Creek.

Page 54.—Tenth line from bottom, read January, 1887, instead of "1877."

GENERAL INDEX.

	PAGES.
Avery Family,	40-42
Brooks Family, of Scituate,	44-51
Brooks, J. B., of Dixon,	18-47
Brooks. Phebe Perkins,	46
Brooks, John Holmes,	47
Brooks, Noah, of Newark, N. J.,	47-51
Camp Family,	30
Camp, Sarah E.,	30
Cutler Family,	38
Curtis Family,	52
Clifton, John, of Salem,	17
Clifton, Hannah U.,	17
Clifton, Sarah Helen,	17
Clifton, J. T. A., of Boston,	17
Gay, Benj. D., of Dixon,	46
Gay, Sarah,	46
Hotten, Lish,	32-36
Kidder Family,	38-40
Little Family, of Plymouth and Marshfield,	42-44
McMaster, Z. J.,	29
Perkins Family, of York,	53-54
Perkins, Joseph, of Castine,	53
Richardson, Samuel, of Woburn,	12

	PAGES.
Southworth Family and English Pedigree,	59-62
Southworth, Constant, of Plymouth,	60
Southworth, Elizur, of Litchfield, Ill.,	62
Southworth, Susan,	30
Upham, John, of Weymouth and Malden,	5-9
Upham, Phineas, of Malden,	9-10
Upham, Thomas, of Reading,	10-11
Upham, Joseph, of Reading and Dudley,	11-13
Upham, Joseph, Jr., of Dudley,	13-14
Upham, Joseph 3d, of Black Creek, N. Y.,	14
Upham, Sylvanus, of Castine,	14-18
Upham, Stranus K., of Dixon,	18-30
Upham, Jeremiah, of Castine,	17
Upham, Frank K., U. S. A.,	30-31
Upham, Chas. C., C., B. & N. Railroad,	28-29
Upham, Margaret B.,	29-30
Upham, Mrs. Marianne,	22-27
Upham, James C., of Nova Scotia,	17
Upham, Cornelia,	17
Upham, Susan,	17
Upham, Frank B,	31
Upham, John Southworth,	31
Upham, Ethelberta,	31
Upham, Edith,	31
Upham, Annie G,	27
Upham, General References of,	9
Wright, Chas. H., of Chicago,	29
Wright, Chas. H. C., of Cambridge,	30
Wright, Marian L.	30
Ware, Peter, of York,	54
Ware Family,	54
Warren, Richard, Pilgrim of the Mayflower,	42
Warren, Richard, Lineage of,	56-59
Wescott, Mary, of Newburyport,	47

www.ingramcontent.com/pod-product-compliance
Lightning Source LLC
Chambersburg PA
CBHW021534270326
41930CB00008B/1248